In loving memory of
Emma Charlotte Young
from
The Vintage Book Club

Animals
on the Farm

Geese

Aaron Carr

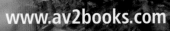

www.av2books.com

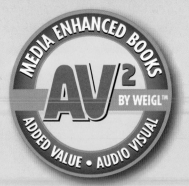

AV² provides enriched content that supplements and complements this book. Weigl's AV² books strive to create inspired learning and engage young minds in a total learning experience.

Your AV² Media Enhanced books come alive with...

Audio
Listen to sections of the book read aloud.

Key Words
Study vocabulary, and complete a matching word activity.

Video
Watch informative video clips.

Quizzes
Test your knowledge.

Embedded Weblinks
Gain additional information for research.

Slide Show
View images and captions, and prepare a presentation.

Try This!
Complete activities and hands-on experiments.

... and much, much more!

Go to **www.av2books.com**, and enter this book's unique code.

BOOK CODE

X720507

AV² **by Weigl** brings you media enhanced books that support active learning.

Published by AV² by Weigl
350 5th Avenue, 59th Floor   New York, NY 10118
Website: www.av2books.com   www.weigl.com

Library of Congress Cataloging-in-Publication Data
Carr, Aaron.
 Geese / Aaron Carr.
   pages cm. -- (Animals on the farm)
 ISBN 978-1-62127-231-1 (hardcover : alkaline paper) -- ISBN 978-1-62127-235-9 (softcover : alkaline paper)
 1. Geese--Juvenile literature. 2. Farm animals--Juvenile literature. I. Title.
 SF505.3.C37 2014
 636.5'98--dc23
                              2012044711

Printed in the United States of America in North Mankato, Minnesota
1 2 3 4 5 6 7 8 9 0   17 16 15 14 13

022013
WEP300113

Senior Editor: Aaron Carr   Art Director: Terry Paulhus

Weigl acknowledges Getty Images as the primary image supplier for this title.

Animals on the Farm

Geese

CONTENTS

3

I am a small farm animal.
Farmers keep me for food
and for my eggs.

5

I am a bird. I have wings, feathers, and a long neck.

I have wings, but I can not fly. I walk and run on my two legs instead.

9

I have a long, sharp bill.
My long, sharp bill helps me eat.

I eat grasses and other plants. I swallow rocks to help me break down my food.

14

How do I talk to other animals? I "honk" to let them know I am there.

I like to be with other geese. I choose just one mate and stay with it for life.

I lay eggs. I sit on the eggs to keep them warm.

My babies hatch from these eggs.

My babies are called goslings. They hatch after one month.

GOOSE FACTS

These pages provide detailed information that expands on the interesting facts found in the book. These pages are intended to be used by adults to help young readers round out their knowledge of each amazing animal featured in the *Animals on the Farm* series.

Pages 4-5

Farmers keep geese for food and for their eggs. Geese raised for food are called poultry. There are many different geese breeds. The Embden and Toulouse breeds are the two most often found on farms in the United States. Goose eggs are used for food. One goose egg is about the size of two chicken eggs.

Pages 6–7

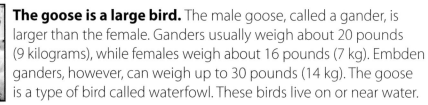

The goose is a large bird. The male goose, called a gander, is larger than the female. Ganders usually weigh about 20 pounds (9 kilograms), while females weigh about 16 pounds (7 kg). Embden ganders, however, can weigh up to 30 pounds (14 kg). The goose is a type of bird called waterfowl. These birds live on or near water.

Pages 8–9

Geese cannot fly. Farm geese are bred to be very large, which makes them too heavy to fly. They move around by walking and swimming. Geese that live in nature are much smaller. They can fly very long distances. These geese fly in large groups arranged in a V-shape.

Pages 10–11

The goose has a long, sharp bill. The goose's bill is wide near the head and narrows toward the tip. This helps the goose pick up food close to the ground. Tiny comblike structures called *lamellae* line the bill. These structures act as a filter to help geese eat food found in water. The tongue is also combed along the edges to help geese eat.

Pages 12–13

Geese eat grass and other plants. Geese eat sedges, weeds, and other plants, but grass is their favorite food. On farms, geese are usually kept in open pastures with a mix of different grasses. One acre (0.4 hectares) of pasture land provides enough space and food for 20 to 40 geese. A goose can digest its food in just 20 minutes.

Pages 14–15

Geese talk by making honking sounds. The honking sound geese make is one of their best-known traits. In nature, geese often make this sound when flying. If a goose becomes angry, it may stand upright, flap its wings, and shake its feathers while honking loudly.

Pages 16–17

Geese stay with the same mate for life. A gander and a goose will often pair with each other for life. When reproducing, both goose parents help take care of their young. Geese usually stay together in large groups. A group of many geese is called a gaggle.

Pages 18–19

Baby geese hatch from eggs. Geese can lay up to 30 eggs in one season. The mother sits on the eggs to keep them warm until they hatch. The father stands guard to protect the nest. Goose eggs hatch about one month after they are laid.

Pages 20–21

Baby geese are called goslings. Goslings stay with their parents for one year after they are born. When they are away from the nest, goslings form a line behind their mother. The father will either walk at the front with the mother or at the back to protect the goslings.

KEY WORDS

Research has shown that as much as 65 percent of all written material published in English is made up of 300 words. These 300 words cannot be taught using pictures or learned by sounding them out. They must be recognized by sight. This book contains 45 common sight words to help young readers improve their reading fluency and comprehension. This book also teaches young readers several important content words. These words are paired with pictures to aid in learning and improve understanding.

Page	Sight Words First Appearance
4	a, am, and, animal, farm, food, for, I, keep, me, my, small
6	have, long
8	but, can, not, on, run, two
10	eat, helps
13	down, other, plants, to
15	do, how, know, let, talk, them, there
17	be, it, just, life, like, one, with
18	the
19	from, these
21	after, are, they

Page	Content Words First Appearance
4	eggs, farmers
6	bird, feathers, neck, wings
8	legs
10	bill
13	grasses, rocks
17	geese, mate
19	babies
21	goslings, month